SOUTHERN REGION ELECTRO DIESEL LOCOMOTIVES AND UNITS

A PICTORIAL SURVEY

SOUTHERN REGION ELECTRO DIESEL LOCOMOTIVES AND UNITS

A PICTORIAL SURVEY

David Cable

PEN & SWORD
TRANSPORT

AN IMPRINT OF PEN & SWORD BOOKS LTD.
YORKSHIRE - PHILADELPHIA

First published in Great Britain in 2019 by
Pen and Sword Transport
An imprint of
Pen & Sword Books Ltd
Yorkshire - Philadelphia

ISBN 978 1 52672 061 0

A CIP catalogue record for this book is available from the British Library.

Typeset by Aura Technology and Software Services, India
Printed and bound in India by Replika Press Pvt. Ltd.

Pen & Sword Books Ltd incorporates the Imprints of Pen & Sword Books Archaeology, Atlas, Aviation, Battleground, Discovery, Family History, History, Maritime, Military, Naval, Politics, Railways, Select, Transport, True Crime, Fiction, Frontline Books, Leo Cooper, Praetorian Press, Seaforth Publishing, Wharncliffe and White Owl.

For a complete list of Pen & Sword titles please contact

PEN & SWORD BOOKS LIMITED
47 Church Street, Barnsley, South Yorkshire, S70 2AS, England
E-mail: enquiries@pen-and-sword.co.uk
Website: www.pen-and-sword.co.uk

or
PEN AND SWORD BOOKS
1950 Lawrence Rd, Havertown, PA 19083, USA
E-mail: Uspen-and-sword@casematepublishers.com
Website: www.penandswordbooks.com

Contents

Introduction

In line with the traditions of the Southern Region of British Railways, the electro-diesel range of locomotives and multiple units were unique to this area, incorporating the facility to work in multiple with other classes used in that region. The designs incorporated two classes of locomotives and essentially four types of multiple units, all of which are specified below.

The locomotive classes comprised the class 73 and class 74, the latter being conversions from class 71 electric locomotives. The class 73s were seen extensively throughout the region, whilst the class 74 worked primarily on the South Western division. The multiple units were formed of classes 201 to 203 for Hastings line services, and classes 204 –207 for local stopping services, which were seen throughout Hampshire, Sussex and parts of Kent.

Class 73

The 49 locos in this class were built between 1962 and 1967, the first six at Eastleigh, the remaining 43 at English Electric's Vulcan Foundry. A Bo-Bo design, they were formed into two sub-groups – 73/0 or JA and 73/1 or JB. The former had an 80mph maximum speed with 1420 electrical HP and a 600 HP English Electric diesel engine. The 73/1s had a 90mph maximum speed and electric power of 1600 HP. The class was originally numbered E6001-49, but after the introduction of TOPS, the JAs became 73001-6 and the JBs 73101-42, one loco having been scrapped after an accident.

Electrical pick-up was by 3rd rail current collectors. The internal wiring system was such that at breaks in the conductor rail (where the voltage could vary due, for example, to voltage drops caused by other traffic) spectacular arcing could occur. This could cause local fires, and when the class was first used on Gatwick Express services leaving Victoria, the fires necessitated using pairs of the class working under diesel power, until fire guards could be fitted around the conductor shoes.

The diesel engine provided the means for the class to be used on non-electrified tracks, or when power was switched off during maintenance work. In 2013/14, seven of the class were re-engined with Cummins and MTU diesels, increasing the power output to 1500/1600 HP respectively. These have been reclassified as 73/9s.

The class has a facility for multiple working, and apart from being compatible with virtually all other Southern Region locos and multiple units, can also work in conjunction with locos of types 2, 3 and 4 from other regions.

Their duties have covered all types of train operation, and in particular have been first choice for trains provided for the Royal Family and other VIPs Twelve of the class were reclassified in 1984 as 73/2s in order to work Gatwick Express services to and from Victoria in push-pull mode. In the late 1980s, when the class 442s were being built using motors from class 432 4REPs, single units replaced a driving coach to for a class 432/9 formed of the 73 and 3 4REP coaches. Others were used in pairs on South Western trains from Waterloo to Bournemouth with 4TC sets.

Much work was undertaken on departmental duties, such as spoil trains from Godstone tip to Tonbridge, and mail and parcels services to and from Tonbridge and Dover to Wembley and Redhill.

Of particular note was their use operating the prestige Orient Express Pullman services in Kent and to Bournemouth/Beaulieu. Two locomotives were acquired to work as Thunderbird locos, able to rescue a failed Eurostar train, for which they were fitted with Scharfenberg couplings. Their range of activity had now become even more widespread with their use in the Midlands and especially on

Caledonian Sleeper services from Edinburgh, which takes them as far afield as Aberdeen Inverness and Fort William.

Following the privatisation of British Rail, the class has been devolved into several ownerships as follows

English, Welsh and Scottish Railways
Eurostar
South West Trains
FM Rail/Fragonset
Southern (73202)
G.B Railfreigh
Merseyrail
Network Rail
Transmart Trains

For a class of 48 locos, they have carried a surprisingly large number of livery variations, as shown below

Green with white stripe
BR Monastral Blue
BR Large Logo
Inter City – 2 versions
Gatwick Express – 2 versions

Network South East
Departmental Grey
Departmental 'Dutch' Grey and Yellow
Network Blue – 2 versions
South West Trains/Stagecoach – 2 versions
Pullman
Merseyrail Yellow
Network Rail
Mainline Blue
EWS
GB Railfright
First GB Railfreight
Fragonset
Southern (73202)
Transmart Blue (73136)
Caledonian Sleeper

The class 73/0s were never named, but many of the rest of the class carried a wide selection. Those allocated to Gatwick Express services carried names of the counties served and associated locations; various universities, locations, festivals and celebrations were included, as well as *The Royal Alex Hospital* and *Oliver Bulleid*.

Class 73 73002 enters Deepcut with a cement train from Blue Circle Northfleet to their depot at Mount Pleasant, Southampton in August 1974.

The special train used on the wedding day of Prince Charles and Princess Diana passes Winchfield in July 1981, on its way from Waterloo to Romsey. The loco is 73142 *Broadlands*, the last vehicle being the SR General Manager's saloon. Note the headcode.

The Brighton Festival Belle leaves Victoria in May 1982 with newly named 73101 *Brighton Evening Argus* at the head of the train.

In June 1982, a visit was made to this country by the Pope. A special train from Gatwick Airport to Victoria was arranged, and is seen passing Clapham Junction behind 73142 *Broadlands*, flying appropriate flags and with a special headcode. One is hesitant to say it, but the cleaners at Stewarts Lane did an even better job on Broadlands for the Pope than they do for HM The Queen.

The Orient Express to Folkestone pulls out of Victoria in the hands of class 73 73113 in August 1982. I worked in the tall office building one floor from the top, but unfortunately it was almost impossible to see down to the station, so I had to do my duties instead!

A Weymouth Quay to Waterloo Channel Islands Boat train speeds out of the sun and passes Hook in September 1982, being worked by 73140.

In October 1982, an unrecorded class 73 passes Basingstoke with the Saturday Bevois Park to Halling Tunnel Cement empties.

A misty November 1982 day sees 73138 near Basing whilst working the daily Eastleigh to Clapham Junction van train.

73138 is seen again, this time hauling two empty coaches from Eastleigh to Clapham Junction in January 1983. The location is near Elvetham, between Winchfield and Fleet.

Having been kicked off Micheldever station by an irate station master (and I am not going to explain why), I took recourse to the road bridge to record 73142 *Broadlands* heading the royal train taking HM The Queen to Portsmouth Harbour in August 1983.

In March 1984, the Southern Electric Group organised a convoluted tour using two class 73s in the then new large logo livery, 73126 and 73138. The train is seen here passing Whitchurch, on a section of line which very rarely saw this class.

The train has now reached Southampton having traversed the Laverstock loop. It is seen entering Southampton West Docks. The cyclist can hardly wait!

Inter City colours have now arrived, and 73123 appropriately named *Gatwick Express* is seen at Victoria in a prototype scheme at the head of a Gatwick Express service. My apologies for leaving my suitcase and the door open!

Large logo 73138 emerges from the Popham tunnels into the chalk surroundings at Micheldever in June 1984, with a southbound departmental service.

An unidentified class 73 scurries along the line from Fareham to Eastleigh with the Fratton to Clapham Junction vans. It is seen in June 1984 near Botley.

Large Logo 73133 is not hanging around as it passes Wandsworth Common on its way from Victoria to Gatwick Airport in August 1984.

Another service to Gatwick Airport in August 1984 approaches Clapham Junction hauled by 73123 in its special Inter City scheme.

More of the class 73s are now being named. Still in blue, 73121 *Croydon* is seen on the Quarry line at Merstham in February 1985 on its way from Victoria to Gatwick Airport.

A lunchtime visit to Victoria in April 1985 coincided with the first birthday of Gatwick Express services. With suitable headboard, 73142 *Broadlands* stands at the head of the train, showing its very short lived high position for its numbers.

An ABS service approaches St. Denys in May 1985, being worked by 73140. The cement tanks at the front are from Northfleet, destined for the Blue Circle Southampton depot at Mount Pleasant.

Light engine 73141 trundles along the line through Chandlers Ford and is seen at Halterworth in June 1985.

The modelmakers are catered for in this shot of 73123 *Gatwick Express* in its prototype Inter City colours, seen on display in July 1985 at the GW 150th open day at Cardiff Canton shed.

The Bevois Park to Halling cement empties climb the bank to the flyover at Battledown behind 73102 *Airtour Suisse* in July 1985. Somewhat of a comedown for a Gatwick Express allocated loco!

A broadside view of a JA class 73, in this case 73003, passing Basingstoke with the Bevois Park to Halling empties in January 1986.

February 1986 and snow still on the ground at Quarry tunnel, where 73125 *Stewarts Lane 1860-1985* propels a Gatwick Express towards Victoria as a down 4CIG unit emerges.

73141 approaches Wokingham in June 1986 with the lightly loaded Tonbridge to Reading vans.

The 25th Anniversary open day at Chart Leacon in June 1986 laid on a shuttle service between the depot and Ashford station. It was operated by 73134 *Woking Homes* with a 4VEP unit.

The Orient Express homebound from Folkestone to Victoria climbs the bank from Tonbridge and is seen approaching Polhill tunnel behind Large Logo 73140 in July 1986.

During the period when the 4REPs were being withdrawn and class 73s replaced some of them, an unrecorded class 73 brings a diverted Weymouth to Waterloo express through Guildford in March 1987. Note that the front TC set now incorporates a buffet car.

A Bournemouth to Waterloo 4REP substitute hauled by 73104 is seen accelerating away from Basingstoke and passing Basing in May 1987.

A Bournemouth to Waterloo express pulls to a stop at Southampton Parkway in the capable hands of Inter City liveried 73107. The date is July 1987. Technically, this is Mainline livery, not Inter City, since it does not carry the Inter City branding.

ED number 73108 shunts a class 421 4 CIG unit across the throat of Brighton station in September 1987.

In January 1988, the SEG excelled itself for rare mileage, when a special destined eventually for Seaford, travelled down the remaining stump of the Gosport branch. Seen here at Fort Brockhurst are 73116 and 73121 *Croydon*, having propelled the stock to the end of the line.

The train now returns and is seen approaching Fareham with 73116 leading 73121 *Croydon*. Needless to say that for such a rare event, the weather that day was unrelenting rain!

An express to Waterloo is ready to leave Bournemouth in March 1988, with 73130 at the head of the train.

A Weymouth to Waterloo express starts away from Southampton Central in April 1988. 73126 has replaced a 4REP motor coach; the remaining three coaches of the set are now classified 432/9.

Another picture showing the 73 with 432/9 combination as 73136 passes Lymington Junction on its way from Weymouth to Waterloo in May 1988.

73118 *Romney Hythe and Dymchurch Railway* propels its train from Waterloo to Poole and is about to enter the north end of Wallers Ash tunnel. May 1988.

In the later version of Inter City colours with full yellow ends, 73205 *London Chamber of Commerce* passes Salfords in August 1988, on its way from Victoria to Gatwick Airport.

A Waterloo to Bournemouth Pullman special approaches Winchfield in September 1988, headed by 73006 in Large Logo livery.

Celebrations are afoot on the Mid Hants line in September 1988. An Alresford to Waterloo special passes Bentley behind 73106.

This is followed by the Watercress Belle to and from Waterloo, powered by 73005 *Mid Hants/Watercress Line* decorated in NSE blue, and looking very smart approaching Bentley.

The Watercress Belle is seen on its return from Waterloo to Alresford at Isington. September 1988.

In November 1988, a Bournemouth to Manchester inter-regional express nears Bramley, very unusually hauled by 73130 *City of Portsmouth* running on its diesel engine. I believe this train used the Reading West curve, so where were the 73 replaced, since relief locos were few and far between, I hate to think – Birmingham??

A Pullman special from Waterloo to Bournemouth passes the head of Southampton Water at Totton, behind 73210 *Selhurst* in December 1988.

Some of the 4REP replacements now have pairs of class 73s to work them, as illustrated here at Waterloo where 73111 and 73135 will shortly depart for Poole in January 1989.

A departmental service clatters (and with these wagons, I mean clatters!) over Farlington Junction in April 1989, making its way towards Portsmouth. The loco is 73117 *University of Surrey*.

A trainload of stone arrives at the yard at Chichester in April 1989, headed by 73138 *Post Haste* in the later Inter City livery.

In NSE blue, 73004 *The Bluebell Railway* passes Fishbourne Junction with the Lavant to Drayton stone train in May 1989. The loco is in a different version of the blue scheme to that seen on 73005 elsewhere. This service was the shortest bulk train load working on BR at that time – and since.

Later that month, 73004 has moved to Waterloo, where it serves as station pilot, being parked with another of the class.

Class 73 73006 arrives at Hoo junction, its destination, in August 1989 with an empty train from Shakespeare Cliff, which, when loaded, has carried segments for the Channel Tunnel.

On Saturdays, the Plymouth to Portsmouth Harbour train was extended to Brighton, with an engine change at Portsmouth. Now in the hands of 73105, it is seen passing Farlington Junction in September 1989.

A Victoria to Gatwick Airport express passes Coulsdon North in January 1990, headed by 73209. The locos allocated to these services had been renumbered in a 73/2 series. The parcels unit was not identified.

The unique blue nameplate identifies the loco as 73202 *Royal Observer Corps*, which speeds towards Victoria from Gatwick Airport, seen near Hooley in January 1990.

April 1990, and a semi-fast service from Bournemouth to Waterloo worked by 73109 with two NSE 4TC sets, passes Basing in nice spring sunshine.

A service from Victoria approaches Gatwick Airport in August 1990, headed by 73211 *County of West Sussex*. This is a summer service made up to eight coaches.

In new Network South East colours, 73109 *Battle of Britain50th Anniversary* passes Wichfield with a special working from St. Denys to Waterloo, comprising one 5-car and one 4-car TC. September 1990.

The special train established for testing the bogies for the Eurostar trains, is seen passing Wnchfield in September 1990. It comprises a semi-fixed formation of an RTC 4TC set, ex-33115 now 83301 and 73205 *London Chamber of Commerce*. It is heading from Eastleigh to Stewarts Lane depot.

In the dull plain grey departmental livery. 73136 is seen at Potbridge with a Waterloo to Southampton semi-fast service in September 1990.

73109 *Battle of Britain 50th Anniversary* is seen with another St. Denys to Waterloo working, this time in February 1991, having just crossed over Battledown flyover.

Potbridge is the location again, this time in August 1991, when sparkling clean 73136 *Kent and East Sussex* passed by with a down departmental working.

A departmental service bound for Three Bridges approaches Gatwick Airport behind 73131 *County of Surrey*, which now carries departmental 'Dutch' yellow and grey colours. September 1991.

Special permission was granted to me to visit Stewarts Lane depot to take a selection of shots of 73101 *Brighton Evening Argus* in its newly applied Pullman livery in November 1991.

73131 *County of Surrey* stands at Sheerness in March 1992 with a mixture of steel scrap and ballast empties.

A set of long welded rails from Tonbridge to Hoo Junction passes Cuxton in June 1992, hauled by 73134 *Woking Homes*.

A Woking to Eastleigh departmental working ambles past Winchfield in July 1992 behind 73107.

Posed on the stabling siding at Redhill in August 1992, nicely cleaned 73129 *City of Winchester* displays its Network South East colours, nameplate and crest for the model makers.

Passing South Acton in November 1992, an Ashford to Willesden departmental service is hauled by 73106 in austere plain grey.

Now carrying the Inter City brand name, 73206 *Gatwick Express* passes Factory Junction with a diverted Victoria to Gatwick Airport express in November 1991. It is interesting to work out how it gets south of Croydon.

A departmental working from Willesden comprising one loaded ballast hopper and three empties passes Barnes in November 1992. The loco is 73105.

A Poole to Waterloo special comprised of the two 4TC sets restored to their original plain blue, passes Winchfield with 73136 *Kent Youth Music* bringing up the rear. November 1992.

A Victoria to Weymouth special passes Bedhampton in December 1992, worked by 73204 *Stewarts Lane 1860-1985*. The white cross on the third coach intrigues me.

The Channel Tunnel bogie test train passes West Byfleet on a frosty morning in December 1992, with 72205 *London Chamber of Commerce* leading 83301. Note that the original RTC 4TC has been expanded to a 6-car set. It is working from Eastleigh to Clapham yard.

The test train is seen again on its return trip to Eastleigh, this time being seen at Byfleet and New Haw station.

An up departmental service heads away from Basingstoke station behind 73134 *Woking Homes* in March 1993.

In full Inter City livery, extra clean 73202 *Royal Observer Corps* passes Raynes Park in March 1993, with Class 421 1314 ECS in tow. Where it was travelling from and to is not known, possibly Eastleigh to Clapham, but if so, why loco hauled?

A final shot of the Channel Tunnel bogie test train, now seen working from Eastleigh to Clapham yard passing Weybridge in March 1993. 73205 *London Chamber of Commerce* leads 83301 and the 6TC set.

April 1993 at Havant saw The Peter Curtis Tribute from London Bridge to Portsmouth Harbour arrive behind 73003. The loco had been restored to the original green colours, named *Sir Herbert Walker* and had the original number E6003 applied. The train was formed of the two all-blue 4TC sets.

Action at Tonbridge West Yard where 73136 *Kent Youth Music* is backing a departmental service to Willesden into the station. A good selection of motive power is present, comprising class 73s, 08s and a 47. April 1993.

The Willesden bound departmental now starts the climb to Polhill and leans to the sharply canted curve as it leaves Tonbridge station.

A Redhill to Tonbridge departmental train passes Godstone in July 1993, worked by 73104. Note the variation in platform height near the signal.

73119 *Kentish Mercury* and 73129 *City of Winchester* are about to cross the Uckfield branch near Edenbridge with a Godstone Tip to Tonbridge spoil train in June 1993.

Pathfinder's DC Green Flasher from Waterloo to Waterloo is seen near Chertsey in July 1993 with 73139 and 72141 in charge at the front.

An against the light shot at a location not normally known these days for locomotives, New Cross. 73104 and 73136 *Kent Youth Music* heads towards central London in November 1993.

E6003/73003 *Sir Herbert Walker* poses broadside on at the open day at Old Oak Common in March 1994.

One of the class 73s transferred to the Merseyrail lines, 73006, is parked at Hall Road one evening in April 1994. Apart from carrying Merseyrail colours and logo, it is also captioned Regional Railways.

Class 73s were used by Eurostar to move their class 373s under alternative means to their own power. In this view at Sandling in July 1994, 73140 and 73107 *Redhill 1844-1984* are bracketed by a pair of Translator wagons, heading west.

Gatwick Express adopted a slight variation to the former Inter City livery using a slightly different shade of red stripe and a new logo. In these new colours, 73207 *County of East Sussex* passes Coulsdon North with a service to the Airport in July 1994.

A Southampton to Waterloo Pullman train passes Winchfield in August 1994, hauled appropriately by Pullman liveried 73101, now renamed *The Royal Alex*. A class 442 intrudes.

A Stewarts Lane-Windsor-Alton-Stewarts Lane track recording train is seen on the Windsor branch near Staines, with 73119 *Kentish Mercury* on the front end. Seen in February 1995.

The train is then caught at Ascot, now showing 73101 *The Royal Alex* at the rear starting to head down the line through Bagshot and Camberley. A somewhat humdrum duty for such a prestige loco!

The Royal Alex, 73101, passes the rear of the signal box at Tonbridge as it commences the journey of the parcels service from Tonbridge to Glasgow in August 1995.

The Tonbridge to Glasgow parcels train is now seen at Edenbridge, now in the hands of 73114 Stewarts Lane 1860-1985, which has acquired the new blue version of Mainline colours. February 1996.

A track recording train heads away west from Woking in July 1996, with 73129 *City of Winchester* bringing up the rear, 73119 *Kentish Mercury* being in front.

A Victoria to Gatwick Airport express speeds past the junctions at Earlswood in July 1996, headed by 73211 in the designated colours adopted for these services.

73107 *Redhill 1844-1994* runs at its maximum speed through Godstone in July 1996, on its way to its namesake town for an engine change, with the Tonbridge to Glasgow parcels service.

Eurostar took over two class 73s for train rescue, which were fitted with Scharfenberg couplings. One of them, 73130 passes Wandsworth Road in September 1996 on an Ashford to North Pole driver training run. Note the three roundels on the right-hand end of the loco, the opposite end to that on other Eurostar stock with these emblems.

Mainline liveried 73114 *Stewarts Lane 1860-1985* enters Redhill in September 1996, with a Tonbridge to Edinburgh parcels service.

The Battersea skyline shows up well as seen from Wandsworth Road, where 73119 *Kentish Mercury* passes by with a track recording train. October 1996. Note the Eurostar service which has departed from Waterloo International.

Privatisation arrives on the scene, and one of the earliest locos to demonstrate it is 73109 *Battle of Britain 50th Anniversary* now in pristine South West Trains colours. It stands in platform 6 at Woking in October 1996.

The morning Eastleigh to Hoo Junction departmental train has seen a wide variety of motive power over the years. In November 1996, it was worked by Mainline 73133 *The Bluebell Railway*, seen in this view at Potbridge.

More track recording work for the 73s, this time at Millbrook in March 1997. On the front is Dutch liveried 73107 *Redhill 1844-1994* ....

.... and bringing up the rear is Mainline liveried 73114 *Stewarts Lane 1860-1985*.

The other loco used by Eurostar, 73118, rune light engine from Stewarts Lane to Ashford, and is seen at Borough Green in April 1997. The Scharfenberg coupling certainly mars the front end.

An interesting pairing at Potbridge, where one of the two class 73s painted in EWS colours, leads Gatwick Express coloured 73212 *Airtour Suisse* and three GE coaches working from Eastleigh to Stewarts Lane in April 1997.

EWS 73131 brings 73206 Gatwick Express light engines up the long straight from Basingstoke and passes Newnham in July 1997. They are working from Eastleigh to Stewarts Lane.

It is all action at Coulsdon North, where Gatwick Expresses meet. Heading for Victoria are 73210 *Selhurst* and 73202 *Royal Observer Corps,* whilst working down to Gatwick is 73207. September 1997.

It is not very often one finds a locomotive at the buffers on the Brighton side of Victoria, but here is EWS 73131 posed for the camera in March 1998. What was it doing? Well, the experimental class 424 was just in front of it, so it had probably brought that into the station for display.

An Orient Express tour from Victoria to Folkestone heads away from Otford Junction in April 1999, worked by Dutch liveried 73105.

Action at Purley in August 2000, where 73204 propels a Gatwick Express towards Victoria, running parallel on the slow lines is an Ardingly to Acton empty stone train, and in the distance, another Gatwick Express squeezes between as it heads south.

73207 works a Victoria bound Gatwick Express comprised of Continental Air coloured coaches. It is passing South Croydon in August 2000.

The other EWS liveried member of the class 73s, 73128, backs out of the yards at Clapham Junction with a Serco test train. March 2001.

South West Trains 73109 *Battle of Britain 50th Anniversary* is at the rear of empty stock about to leave Woking for Wimbledon in May 2001.

Mainline 73133 *The Bluebell Railway* brings up the rear of a Wembley Railnet to Dover TPO, which is passing Kensington Olympia in July 2003. The train is headed by 73136 *Kent Youth Music*.

The same pair of locos, but with 73133 now on the front, pass Reedham Sidings at Coulsdon North, with a similar service a few days later.

Warnham, north of Horsham, on a typical murky November day in 2004 is the setting for a Victoria to Chichester special hauled by a pair of GB Railfreight liveried members of the class, 73204 *Janice* and 73206 *Alison*.

Of all the places to see a pair of class 73s, Pudding Mill Lane must be amongst the most unusual, but in February 2005, a special from Crewe to Southend via Liverpool Street passed with GBRf 73205 *Jeanette* and 73204 *Janice* heading the train. Of course, a DLR train had to enter the platform at the crucial moment!

South West Trains acquired 73201 to serve as a Thunderbird loco, and it was decorated in a Stagecoach based colour scheme. Seen here near Chalton in June 2005, it followed a last slam door stock trip to Weymouth by a class 423 and 421, just in case of any problems.

Now viewed at closer quarters, 73201 passes Millbrook on a Poole to Eastleigh driver training run, using one of the Lymington branch 3-car sets. August 2005.

Having gone from Eastleigh to Fareham, 73201 returns past Millbrook returning to Poole for driver training later that same day.

April 2006 saw a special from Victoria visit Littlehampton. On the approach to the town, blue liveried 73136 *Perseverance* hauled the train ....

..........whilst Fragonset liveried 73107 brought up the rear.

After the visit to Littlehampton, the train moved on to Bognor Regis, with Fragonset 73107 now leading as it arrives at the resort..........

..................and 73136 *Perseverance* trails at the rear end of the train.

Network Rail took over two of the class, which are seen here stabled at Tonbridge West yard. Numbered 73213 and 73212, they carry their new owner's yellow colours. June 2006.

73202 was designated as a Thunderbird loco for Gatwick Express services and painted in a special colour scheme. It is seen passing Clapham Junction in May 2009, hauling a class 442 EMU from Lovers Walk to Victoria, from whence it presently returned.

In May 2009, Potbridge witnessed 73109, now in the new Stagecoach colours, hauling green liveried class 421 1498, one of the Lymington branch units, from Bournemouth to Wimbledon.

With 66712 on the front end, a special working the leg from Littlehampton to Ardingly, passes Angmering in October 2010, with 73141 in First GBRf colours doing its duty at the rear.

A railhead treatment train passes Winchfield station in December 2010, fronted by First GBRf 73212, 73141 being towed at the rear.

Class 73s are seen in profusion at Potbridge in October 2013. From the front they are 73212/136/141,119,206/207, at least three having been repainted from previous schemes. They were working from Tonbridge to Eastleigh.

The Thunderbird loco, 73202, has now been taken over by the Southern franchise, painted accordingly and named *Dave Berry*. It is passing Clapham Junction in March 2014, working light from Littlehampton to Stewarts Lane. *(Ian Francis)*

Network Rail's 73137 passes St. Denys in January 2016 with a test train from Weymouth to Eastleigh. *(Ian Francis)*

Now being used by Caledonian Sleepers, 73968 passes Haymarket in March 2016, with the empty sleeper stock from Edinburgh Waverley to Polmadie for servicing. *(Ian Francis)*

Two of the re-engined class 73s are caught working a Crewe to Derby departmental train passing Stenson Junction in May 2016. Leading is GBRf 73963 *Janice*.........

..............whilst on the back is 73962 *Dick Mabbutt*.

73968 stands in Aberdeen station in May 2017at the head of the Caledonian Sleeper to Edinburgh and Euston. *(Ian Francis)*

Class 74

The ten electro-diesel locomotives of class 74 were rebuilds of surplus class 71 all-electric engines used on the South Eastern section. The work was undertaken at Crewe in 1967-8. The electric power output was 2552 HP and the Paxman diesel generated 650 HP. The diesel engine proved somewhat unreliable in service. A maximum speed of 90mph was specified, although speeds in excess of 100mph were recorded.

The intention was to provide a locomotive with higher power output and maximum speed, which would enable them to handle the boat trains to and from Southampton Docks, and to avoid engine changes at Bournemouth when working boat trains to and from Weymouth. In the event, it was decided not to operate on diesel power to Weymouth, since a failure of the diesel engine on the single line sections west of Poole would cause chaos. There were also doubts about whether the diesel power was of sufficient capacity to haul a Channel Islands boat train up the bank to Bincombe Tunnels, and up Parkstone bank. They would also be used on other Bournemouth line passenger trains, mail and parcels services, and could also be seen on West London milk and freight transfer services.

Like the class 73s, they were compatible with other Southern Region stock for multiple working, although this was rare in practice. The locos had an early form of electronic train control specifically to minimise wheel slip. However, such a concept was still in its infancy and did cause reliability problems.

By 1976, cruise ship numbers had reduced, as had freight and parcels work, and although the electronic control problems could, by that time, have probably been overcome, the shortage of work could not justify their retention, and by the end of 1977, they were all scrapped.

The class 74s were originally numbered in an E series – E6101-E6110 – becoming 74001-74010 under the TOPS system. They were only seen in BR Monastral blue, and none were named.

Carrying its original number E6101 (74001) stands at Crewe Works in February 1968, awaiting commissioning at Stewarts Lane. *(Colin Marsden)*

E6104 (74004) stands in the sidings at Clapham Junction in April 1968. This view shows what a neat design this, and the class 71s, were.
(DC Collection)

A Waterloo to Weymouth express passes Potbridge in October 1970, hauled by 74007. The train is formed of two 4TC sets. *(DC Collection)*

A Southampton Docks to Waterloo boat train enters Waterloo station in August 1974, headed by 74002.

A pair of class 74s, 74003 and 74008, are stabled in the sidings alongside the old Windsor line platforms at Waterloo. August 1974.

74001 has passed Pirbright Junction and enters Deepcut in August 1974, working west with a short van train for the Bournemouth line.

74002 stands in Wimbledon West Yard waiting to leave with the Wimbledon to Tolworth coal train in June 1975. *(Colin Marsden)*

The Eastleigh to Clapham vans pass Brookwood behind 74005 on a very overcast day in July 1975.

A short van train for Southampton East Docks passes Winchfield, worked by 74003 in March 1976. *(DC Collection)*

74001 stands at Staines in November 1976 with a Waterloo to Waterloo parcels service via Twickenham and Richmond. *(Colin Marsden)*

A Weymouth Quay to Waterloo boat train passes Surbiton in September 1977, hauled by 74010. *(Colin Marsden)*

74005 passes Eastleigh with a Waterloo to Weymouth Quay boat train on an unknown date. *(Rail Photoprints)*

The scrap lines at Eastleigh in March 1978 contained several of the class 74s. In the front of these four, 74002 awaits its end.

Classes 201, 202 and 203

These three classes can be considered together, since the concept of the design was identical and there were only relatively minor differences between them. The restricted gauge through the tunnels of the line between Tonbridge and Hastings had always required rolling stock to be of narrower dimensions than that used elsewhere, and when steam was due to finish working on this line, a special design of new diesel-powered stock was required.

These three classes were built to a narrow body width in the mid-1950s. Each unit comprised six coaches, formed of two motor coaches each with a 500 HP English Electric diesel engine, with four trailer coaches in between them. The class 201 was categorised 6S, having coaches 56ft 11in long, the class 202 6L with coaches 63ft 5in long, and the similar 6B having a buffet car in place of one of the trailer vehicles. Twenty-three sets were built, seven being class 201, nine being class 202 and seven class 203. They had a maximum speed of 75mph. They could work in multiple with classes 201 to 207.

A reduction in services on this line resulted in three units being used elsewhere (see class 206). The major accident at Hither Green in November 1967 also saw coaches from the units involved being scrapped, although the motor coaches were repaired.

The classes were popular with enthusiasts undertaking special tours, and one set has been retained, a four car set augmented with a standard width buffet car, which has been rostered on regular service trains.

The trains originally appeared in BR green followed by BR blue and finally blue and grey. The preserved unit has been restored to green.

Class 202 1017 arrives at Charing Cross in July 1975, with a service from Hastings. The Shell Tower fills the right-hand side.

Class 202 1016 comes round the curve from Borough Market Junction and arrives at London Bridge with a Hastings bound train in July 1975.

A service from Hastings to Charing Cross leaves London Bridge in July 1975, with class 202 1012 forming the rear of a twelve car train.

The train seen in the previous picture has now arrived and departed again from Charing Cross and passes London Bridge on its way to Hastings. July 1975.

Bound for Hastings from Charing Cross, class 201 1006 approaches Chiselhurst in March 1980.

Caught completely by surprise at a location that I never expected to see one of the class, class 201 1003 brings up the rear of a high-speed test train seen passing Swaythling in June 1985.

A wet day at Dunton Green in July 1985 witnesses class 202 1016 working a 12-car Cannon Street to Hastings service....................

...................with class 201 1004 forming the rear six cars.

The Somerset and Avon Hastings DEMU Railtour, organised by the Southern Electric group, rushes through Andover on its way west in October 1985, class 202 1017 forming the train.

A misty autumn morning in November 1985 catches class 201 1004 climbing towards the entrance to Polhill Tunnel with a Hastings to Cannon Street train.

At the same location now in March 1986, class 201 1006, leading a 12-car train, has nearly reached Polhill Tunnel with a Cannon Street bound train from Hastings.

The Hastings units were useful for running tours on lines with low axle loadings, although in this case not needed. Class 201 1007 brings up the rear working along the Ludgershall branch in the course of a Branch Line Society tour in March 1986.

The BLS tour seen in the previous picture is now seen near Warminster with class 201s 1005 and 1007 forming the train.

The BLS tour reaches its destination, Merehead, and is seen in the unique company of Foster Yeoman's SW1001 44 Western Yeoman and new class 59 59003. March 1986.

Class 201 leader 1001 heads towards London near Polhill in April 1986, with a Hastings to Cannon Street service.

With the withdrawal of the classes 201-3 approaching, farewell tours start to be organised. This one comprising class 201 1002 and class 203 1032 was seen passing Crowthorne in May 1986.

Now renumbered with a TOPS designation, units 203001 and 202001form the Hastings DEMU Swansong tour, which was seen passing Potbridge in August 1987.

Hastings Diesels Ltd. has preserved one class 201, which is available for hire on the main lines. Augmented by a standard gauge buffet car, set 1001 is seen passing Havant in June 1999 working ECS from Lovers Walk to Fratton.

Of all the places one did not expect to see a Hastings unit, Coedkernew must rank near the top. Class 201 1001 was seen there in November 1999 working a regular Portsmouth Harbour to Cardiff service.

Classes 204 and 205

Following the cessation of steam operated stopping services in the Southern Region, a series of two car diesel units were built from 1957, later becoming augmented to three cars. Originally classified as 2H and 3H, they were seen particularly in Hampshire, Sussex and the Marshlink in Kent. Nicknamed Thumpers because of their distinctive engine noise, they became colloquially known as Hampshire units.

The 600 HP English Electric diesel engine was mounted above floor level, which gave passengers a quieter ride than with underfloor engines, but had the disadvantage of losing some seating capacity. A maximum speed of 75mph enabled them to work some services on main lines such as from Basingstoke to Salisbury, although their acceleration could be described at best as sedentary!

But their main spheres of duties were on the pre-electrified line from Portsmouth to Southampton, and thence to Salisbury, the Mid-Hants line from Alton through to Southampton Terminus, Reading to Basingstoke, Salisbury and Portsmouth Harbour, and in later times the Oxted line services to Uckfield. For a short period in the 1970s, they even operated on the Wylye Valley route from Portsmouth Harbour to Bristol Temple Meads, which must have taxed anyone undertaking the whole trip!

The class 204 version comprised the same characteristics as the class 205, but the additional coach to make a 3-car unit had been an ex-2EPB driving trailer, which had been used with the class 206 DEMUs.

In order to assist platform staff as to which end of the train the luggage compartment was situated, the appropriate end initially carried an orange V, which was replaced by an inverted black triangle when yellow coach ends were adopted.

These classes carried five colour schemes, although not carried by every unit:

BR Green
BR Monastral Blue
BR Blue and Grey
Network South East
Connex South Central

Class 204 1401 approaches Mortimer station through the verdant countryside in June 1983, with a Reading to Portsmouth Harbour working.

A Portsmouth Harbour to Salisbury train rounds the curve into Netley station, with class 204 1402 covering the duty. April 1984.

Unit number 1403 heads away from Cosham station in May 1985 working an Eastleigh to Portsmouth Harbour service.

Snaking round the curves near Netley, 1403 passes by in bright May 1985 sunshine on its way from Romsey to Portsmouth & Southsea.

In the original green with orange V to denote at which end is the luggage compartment, class 205 1110 stops at Dean in August 1964 with a Salisbury to Eastleigh service.

A Portsmouth to Salisbury train operated by set 1124 is seen opposite the sidings at Bevois Park in November 1981.

Unit 1133 thumps away from its stop at Andover whilst working from Reading to Salisbury in June 1984.

An Eastleigh to Portsmouth Harbour train stops at Botley in July 1984, worked by class 205 1128. The Foster Yeoman stone terminal is in the far background.

With elements of the Portsmouth skyline on the horizon, set number 1130 enters Fratton with a Salisbury service from Portsmouth Harbour in May 1985.

Portchester station hosts class 205 1130 which starts away towards its destination, Portsmouth Harbour, in May 1985.

Passing the sidings at Bevois Park, with the Tunnel Cement silo prominent, and a class 08 going about its business, an unidentified class 205 is working from Portsmouth & Southsea to Romsey. May 1985.

Set number 1110 stands at the end of the remaining spur of the Tidworth line at Ludgershall in March 1986. Even for the BLS, this was rare trackage, but some members were upset, because the motor end coach did not allow a few feet of track to be traversed, which would have applied if the unit had been positioned the other way round. Some people!!

Now in Network South East colours, 205032 powers (if that is the right word) away from Mortimer in June 1990, with a Basingstoke to Reading shuttle service.

One of the Marshlink allocated units, 205002, leaves Ashford ECS for servicing at Chart Leacon. April 1991.

Seen near Milborne Wick in May 1992, 205033 is working a Saturday morning Yeovil Junction to Salisbury service. Class 205s were rare beasts west of Gillingham.

One class 205, 205029, was restored to green livery, and is seen in pristine state at Basingstoke in August 1992, having arrived from Reading. Note the yellow edge to the part closed door, a useful safety feature.

205033 trundles along near Freefolk, just east of Whitchurch, making its steady way from Reading to Salisbury in May 1993.

The class 207 Oxted line units have left for pastures new, and class 205s have taken their places. 205023 waits to depart with an Uckfield to East Croydon service in May 1993.

Entering Oxted from the London direction, 205027 will draw to a halt with its train from East Croydon to Uckfield. May 1993.

Class leader 205001 arrives at Nutfield in June 1993, with a Reigate to Tonbridge working. The straight line between Redhill and Tonbridge is very apparent.

205032 works a Tonbridge to Reigate service seen near Edenbridge in June 1993. It is crossing the Uckfield branch, the tunnel of which is opened out to provide clearance for the overbridge.

Now in Connex South Central (CSC) colours, 205018 enters Edenbridge Town station with an Oxted to Uckfield train in May 2000.
One lamp post looks as if it had had a night out!

CSC 205033 stops at Edenbridge Town working from Uckfield to Oxted in May 2000. Note the absence of a black triangle.

CSC 205025 nears the end of its August 2002 journey from Uckfield to East Croydon as it passes South Croydon between stone empties and a Gatwick Express. Note that it is formed of only two cars.

Seen again further down the line, 205025 approaches Ashurst in July 2003 with an Uckfield to Oxted service.

Two-car CSC 205205 stands in Ashurst station whilst working from East Croydon to Uckfield in July 2003. Note the pair of numbers on the front end.

Class 206

By 1964, a reduction in services on the Hastings line resulted in twelve vehicles of classes 201-3, six motor coaches and six trailers becoming available for duties elsewhere.

The line chosen for their use was the North Downs route from Reading to Tonbridge via Guildford and Redhill. In order to equip the trains for this, a driving trailer had to be provided, which came from 2 EPB units. These were of course, standard width coaches, which in conjunction with the other narrow Hastings gauge vehicles, gave rise to their nickname of Tadpole units, which feature is quite clear in photographs.

The driving trailers were modified by having a 3-bay luggage area provided, because of the volume of mail traffic on this route.

The 500 HP English Electric diesel engines were uprated to 600 HP to cope with the increased workload. Maximum speed remained at 75mph.

The class 206 appeared in three colour schemes:

BR Green
BR Monastral Blue
BR Blue and Grey – Hastings coaches only, driving trailer still in all over blue.

With the full width driving trailer leading, Tadpole unit 1206 is seen near Winnersh in May 1974, working from Tonbridge to Reading.

Unit number 1205 arrives at Crowthorne in May 1974, also working from Tonbridge to Reading.

In the harsh light of an August 1975 day, 1206 pauses at Guildford in the midst of a Tonbridge to Reading working.

By April 1979, the two ex-Hastings cars had received a repaint into blue and grey, although the ex 2EPB trailer stayed blue. Illustrating this, 1203 stops at Wokingham on its way from Reading to Tonbridge. The profiles of the difference in width can be seen.

1203 now leaves Wokingham for Tonbridge and demonstrates the curious combination of vehicles forming these units.

A Reading to Tonbridge train is operated by set 1202 seen in April 1979 at Blackwater, with the carriage widths quite apparent.

Set number 1204 stands in Reigate station on an unknown date, with a Reading to Tonbridge service. *(DC Collection)*

Class 207

In 1962, a class of 19 3-car DEMUs were built, of similar characteristics to the class 205, but with a more streamlined front end. These were allocated to the Oxted lines, serving East Grinstead prior to the electrification of that section, and the line serving Uckfield. Occasionally they worked on the Marshlink line in Kent, and through to Tunbridge Wells West.

Following the East Grinstead electrification, several were withdrawn, and a number of the remaining units were transferred to work services from Reading to Basingstoke.

They carried five colour schemes although not carried by every unit:

BR Green
BR Monastral Blue
BR Blue and Grey
Network South East
Connex South Central

A six car train from East Grinstead arrives at Victoria in July 1975. the rear unit being number 1317.

Class 207 1315 leaves Clapham Junction in March 1979 with a pre-electrification service from East Grinstead to Victoria. The 3D sub-classification is clearly marked.

Set 1317 has now moved to work a service to Tonbridge in August 1979. It stands in Reading's old platform 4B, the photo being taken from the site of the old SR station. The range of cars brings back some memories.

A six car train, comprising class 207 1310 and a class 205 (note the positions of first class compartments), leaves Clapham Junction in July 1981 for Victoria, working a service from East Grinstead.

Normally worked by a class 205 Thumper, 207005 was an unusual sight on this Portsmouth Harbour to Gillingham service, seen near Sutton Mandeville in September 1987.

Having just passes Aldershot South Junction, 207008 is nearing Ash as it wends its way from Reading to Tonbridge in October 1987. Who put the cone there?

207010 rounds the curve into Salisbury station, terminating its journey from Waterloo in October 1987.

Now working from Basingstoke to Reading, 207010 is seen near Silchester in April 1988.

207010 certainly gets around. It is now seen working an Eastleigh to Portsmouth Harbour train, approaching Hilsea in April 1989, with a 4VEP disappearing under the walls, and Portsdown filling the skyline.

Yet again, 207010 is the subject, now in NSE colours, with the spire of the church projecting over the trees, the unit is leaving Mortimer behind, as it works from Basingstoke to Reading.

A Salisbury to Reading train arrives at Andover in June 1992, worked by 207017. Note that first class accommodation has now been declassified.

207017 gets full sun treatment in June 1992, as it works a Salisbury to Reading service, seen near Oakley.

Now with its front number repositioned, our old friend 207010 departs from Overton, working from Salisbury to Reading in May 1993. The Portals factory identifies this location very clearly.

Summary

Apart from the few remaining class 73s, none of the electro-diesel locomotives or diesel electric multiple units remain in regular main line service. They performed their duties generally without problems, and on those lines to which they, and in particular the DEMUs, were rostered, they created an ambience which could not be replicated elsewhere.

This album endeavours to illustrate all these classes going about their work in a variety of locations, and in a range of colour schemes. Unless otherwise stated, they are all my own photos. They are arranged by class, and then in date order.

They provide a fitting tribute to a series of unique designs, which served the Southern Region well for many years, and as someone who lives in the south of England, are sorely missed.

David Cable
Hartley Wintney July 2017